Declar

⊃U!

"Speaking into your atmosphere"

Apostle Vanzant Luster

Divinity Kingdom Publishing

Declare and Decree it SO!

Published by Divinity Kingdom
Publishing

Printed by: Creative Space

Written by Vanzant Luster 2013

Copyright © 2013

Acknowledgments

First and foremost, I must give God great honor and glory. I would have never thought that I would be writing my 10th book, so I dedicate this book to my Lord and savior Jesus Christ, who is the bishop and lover of my soul, my hope for tomorrow. I praise God for down - loading within me once again the ability to complete my tenth book. What a great accomplishment at this time of my life.

Content

Introduction

Declare and Decree it SO!

This book provides decrees and daily scriptures for your everyday life and intimate time with the Lord. The purpose for this book is to enhance your prayer life, to strengthen you in your walk with the lord and experience great manifestation in your life.

Remember to watch your thoughts, they will become your words, watch your words, they will become your actions, watch your actions, they will become your habits, watch your habits they will become your character, watch your character, they will become your DESTINY.

As you take the journey throughout this devotional book, I pray that your experience will be satisfying to your soul.

Activate Your Day

I command this day and declare it to be a day of increase and over flow, a day of nothing lacking and nothing broken. I take authority over this day in Jesus name, that every element of the atmosphere shall cooperate with the will of the kingdom for my life on today. My season of frustration and failures are over, and I am now walking in seasons of success and prosperity, in every area of my life. Old things are passed away; and all things have become new.

Divine favor is upon me, and it goes before me to make every crooked place straight, it causes men to do things for me they normally wouldn't do for anyone else.

Anything or anyone assigned to undermine, frustrate, hinder, or hurt me in any way, I command to be moved out of my sphere of influence in the name of Jesus! I declare this day, a day of grace, peace, victory and no weapon formed against me shall prosper.

Sunday Morning

"Speaking Blessings into your atmosphere"

~ Jabez Prayer ~

Jabez cried to the God of Israel, saying, Oh, that You would bless me and enlarge my border, and that Your hand might be with me, and You would keep me from evil so it might not hurt me! And God granted his <u>request</u>.

1 Chronicles 4 (AMP)

I declare the blessings of the Lord shall be upon me to enlarge my territory and increase my borders, His hand is upon me to lead and guide me into all truth and to keep me from evil.

The Lord blesses you (me) and watch, guard, and keeps you; (me) The Lord makes His face to shine upon and enlighten you (me) and be gracious (kind, merciful, and giving favor) to you; (me)

The Lord lifts up His [approving] countenance upon you (me) and gives you (me) peace (tranquility of heart and life continually).

Numbers 6:24-26 (AMP)

I declare that I shall experience uncommon favor to open uncommon doors for uncommon things to happen in my life.

I decree it so, in Jesus name!

Monday Morning

~Kingdom Provision~

And God is able to make all grace (every favor and earthly blessing) come to you in abundance, so that you may always and under all circumstances and whatever the need be self-sufficient possessing enough to require no aid or support and furnished in abundance for every good work and charitable donation.

I declare, that all grace and every favor and earthly blessing will come to me in abundance and over flow, so that I will always under all circumstances have whatever I need to be self-sufficient possessing more then enough to require no assistance or support to furnished in abundance for every good work and charitable donation.

As it is written, He [the benevolent person] scatters abroad; He gives to the poor; His deeds of justice and goodness and kindness and benevolence will go on and endure forever!

I declare, as a benevolence person I shall scatter abroad to give to the poor in goodness and kindness forever, and God shall provide me with seed to sow and multiply my resources for increase that I may have to give bread for eating to those who are in need, for the glory of God.

And [God] who provides seed for the sower and bread for eating will also provide and multiply your [resources for] sowing and increase the fruits of your righteousness which manifests itself in active goodness, kindness, and charity.

Thus you will be enriched in all things and in every way, so that you can be generous, and [your generosity as it is] administered by us will bring forth thanksgiving to God.

For the service that the ministering of this fund renders does not only fully supply what is lacking to the saints (God's people), but it also overflows in many [cries of] thanksgiving to God.

I declare, that I am enriched in all things in every area, so that I am fully able to supply what's lacking to the saints and those who are in need.

Because at [your] standing of the test of this ministry, they will glorify God for your loyalty and obedience to the Gospel of Christ which you confess, as well as for your generous-hearted liberality to them and to all [the other needy ones.

2 Corinthians 9 (AMP)

Personal Notes

"The Lord is my shepherd I shall not want"

Tuesday Morning

~Safety in Obedience~

Lord, you said "If I am willing and obedient. I shall eat the good of the land." Now bless me in my obedience.

1. If you will listen diligently to the voice of the Lord your God, being watchful to do all His commandments which I command you this day, the Lord your God will set you high above all the nations of the earth.

2. And all these blessings shall come upon you and overtake you if you heed the voice of the Lord your God.

3. Blessed shall you be in the city and blessed shall you be in the field.

4. Blessed shall be the fruit of your body and the fruit of your ground and the fruit of your beasts, the increase of your cattle and the young of your flock.

5. Blessed shall be your basket and your kneading trough.

6. Blessed shall you be when you come in and blessed shall you be when you go out.

7. The Lord shall cause your enemies who rise up against you to be defeated before your face; they shall come out against you one way and flee before you seven ways.

8. The Lord shall command the blessing upon you in your storehouse and in all that you undertake. And He will bless you in the land which the Lord your God gives you.

9. The Lord will establish you as a people holy to Himself, as He has sworn to you, if you keep the commandments of the Lord your God and walk in His ways.

10. And all people of the earth shall see that you are called by the name [and in the presence of] the Lord, and they shall be afraid of you.

11. And the Lord shall make you have a surplus of prosperity, through the fruit of your body, of your livestock, and of your ground, in the land which the Lord swore to your fathers to give you.

12. The Lord shall open to you His good treasury, the heavens, to give the rain of your land in its season and to bless all the work of your hands; and you shall lend too many nations, but you shall not borrow.

13. And the Lord shall make you the head, and not the tail; and you shall be above only, and you shall not be beneath, if you heed the commandments of the Lord your God which I command you this day and are watchful to do them.

14. And you shall not turn aside from any of the words which I command you this day, to the right hand or to the left, to go after other gods to serve them.

Deuteronomy 28 (AMP)

Personal Notes

He that dwell (abides) in the secret place of the most High shall abide under the shadow of the almighty.

Wednesday Morning

~Setting your Atmosphere~

I declare this day, that no weapon form against me, my health, mind, body, family, relationships and spiritual family shall prosper, and every assignment and contract of the enemy shall be cancel out in the name of Jesus. I render the plans, schemes, tactics, traps and every diabolical attacks of the enemy, powerless, inoperable, and ineffective against me and those who are connected to me.

I declare every unassigned door to be shut in my life, and every assign appointed door to be open unto me in both the spiritual and natural realm in Jesus name. I release the blood of Jesus over every door entrance, and forbid the enemy from coming back into any area of my life.

I declare that this year, I will encounter great favor and great grace, I will be enlarge, and experience increase in every area of my life, in my going, and coming, in my lying down and rising, in relationships, business, and ministry.

I am now walking in abundance, nothing lacking and nothing broken, I shall walk among those who are divinely connected to the kingdom.

I declare that money will always seek me and fine me, and come into my hands in abundance, so that I will always have to buy whatever I need and desire at anytime. I declare that money will always be in my hand to sow seed into those of the kingdom and give to those in need and charitable donation.

I declare, that whatever my hands set to do will increase and prosper, and everything that is for me, due me, will come to me without delay for I shall receive my portion!

I declare, that my ending shall be greater then my beginning I shall be the head and not the tail.

I decree it so, in the name of Jesus Christ!

Personal Notes

Create in me a clean heart, O God; and renew a right spirit within me. Psalm 51:10

Thursday Morning

~Covering Your Day in the Blood~

13. The blood shall be for a token or sign to you upon [the doorposts of] the houses where you are, [that] when I see the blood, I will pass over you, and no plague shall be upon you to destroy you when I smite the land of Egypt. 14. And this day shall be to you for a memorial.

Exodus 12:13-14

I declare the blood of Jesus, to be cover over my life on today, to protect my going and coming, to shield and keep me from every hurt, harm and danger, accidents seen and unseen.   Let the blood be applied over atmospheres, surroundings, highways, cars, homes, cell phones frequencies, telephones lines, radio broadcast, airwaves, ministries, businesses, schools, finances, relationships, marriages, families, sons, daughters, grandchildren, and every person that's connected to the body of Christ.

Let the blood be against every diabolical power of darkness, principalities, rulers of darkness, spiritual wickedness in high places, witchcraft, voodoo, strongman, spirit of backlash, retaliation, sabotage, accusation, murder, rage, anger, danger seen and unseen, spiritual and natural accidents, suicide, molestation, pornography, sodomy, depression, seduction, evil influence, generational spirits, and the spirit of Jezebel.

I declare that the blood be against every witch, warlock, witch doctor, and satanist. Let every demonic contract assignments be powerless, inoperable, nullify, canceled out and destroyed in the blood. And because of the power of the blood no danger can come nigh my dwelling.

I decree it so, in the name of Jesus Christ!

Friday Morning

~Speaking His Word~

So shall My word be that goes forth out of my mouth; it shall not return to me void... without producing any effect, useless but it shall accomplish that which I please and purpose, and it shall prosper in the thing for which I sent it. Isaiah 55:11 - (Amp)

Therefore, I declare that the words I speak out of my month shall not return unto me void, for I shall have what I say, it shall accomplish without fail and manifest where I send it to.

1. He that dwells in the secret place of the most High shall abide under the shadow of the Almighty.

2. I will say of the Lord, He is my refuge and my fortress: my God; in Him will I trust.

3. Surely He shall deliver me from the snare of the fowler, and from the noisome pestilence.

4. He shall cover me with His feathers, and under His wings shall I trust: His truth shall be my shield and buckler.

5. I shall not be afraid for the terror by night; nor for the arrow that flieth by day.

Father, keep me in your secret place, abiding under the shadow of the almighty. For you are my refuge and my fortress in you I trust, deliver me from the snare of the enemy and from his deadly pestilence. Keep me cover under your wings. Let your truth and buckler be my shield and I shall not be afraid by the terror at night.

6. Nor for the pestilence that walketh in darkness; nor for the destruction that wasteth at noon day.

7. A thousand Shall fall at my side: and ten thousand at my right hand; but it shall not come my dwelling.

8. Only with my eye shall I behold and see the reward of the wicked.

9. Because I have made the Lord, who is my refuge, the most High, my habitation;

10. There shall no evil befall me, neither shall any plague come nigh my dwelling.

11. For He shall give His angels charge over me, to keep me in all my ways.

12. They shall bear me up in their hands, lest I dash my foot against a stone.

Psalms 91(AMP)

Father you are my Lord and refuge, my High priest and my habitation, therefore no evil shall befall me, neither any plague shall come near my dwelling.

For you have given your angels command over me to keep in all my ways. Therefore, I will have no fear of the terror by night, for your angels shall hold me up in their hands.

Saturday Morning

~Decreeing Your Day~

I decree that Jesus Christ is Lord over my life, my thoughts, my decisions, my actions, my imagination, my desires, my homes, my vehicles, my atmosphere, my relationships, my ministries and businesses!

I decree that the, trials, challenges, set backs and failures of my past will no longer hinder the purpose and destiny of my future, for the disappointments and sorrows of my past have built a bridge for me to cross over for a greater future! I declare now, that my latter days shall be greater than my former!

I decree that I am no longer who I used to be, and go to the places I use to go, but I am growing from glory to glory by leaps and bounds everyday becoming the image of Christ for His glory!

I decree that I am whole in spirit, and my body is healthy and strong, my mind is alert and disciplined, and my spirit is sensitive, and receptive to the things of God!

I decree that I am walking out of debt and moving into the place of nothing lacking and nothing broken. I am changing old patterns of reckless habits which caused me financial heart-ship.

I decree that I have uncommon favor for uncommon blessings and results in my life! I am engineered for excellence and greatness, created to conquer and sent to succeed and overcome.

I decree that, sin has no more power over my life! And death has no sting, for I am an over-comer in Christ Jesus, because of the shed blood of Jesus Christ.

I decree and declare now that I shall live and not die, but shall fulfill the call and destiny upon my life. And become everything that I was created to be in Christ Jesus!

Declaring Healing

Father, according to your word, we are heal by your strips, so I declare now that I am healed in my body, mind, soul and in every fiber of my being... I declare that, no infirmity or disease sent by the enemy shall be hidden and remain in any part of my lungs, kidneys, liver, colon, spline, veins, muscles, bones, spine, back, blood stream, red and white blood cells, thyroid, brain cells, and heart. For it has no legal right to dwell in my body.

Father, teach and show me how to choose the correct foods that I should eat for my blood type, foods that will keep my body healthy and whole. Father, give me the mind to exercise in order to keep my body strong and mobile, also the mind to read to keep my mental capacity alert and aware. Thank you father for long life and good health. I decree it so in the blood of the Lamb. Amen.

Personal Notes

My soul, wait thou only upon God; for my expectation is from him. Psalms 61:5

Offenses

Father, forgive me of all offense from pass, present, knowingly and unknowingly.

Out of ignorance I have openly walked in the spirit of offense which caused, sickness, breech births, miscarriages in my relationships, ministry and life, Father cut every spirit of offense that's still tied and lingers to my soul from broken divorces, relationships, friendships, ministries, and business connections. Father, help me from this day forward to recognize this spirit, so that, I will no longer be in its grips of offense.

I decree that I will no longer be held captive to any pass offenses and its stronghold side affects, which causes spiritual blockage, break-ups, delays, set backs, division, hindrances, separations, emotional sickness, misunderstandings, confusion and disturbance in my life.

I decree now, it will no longer affect my present relationships, friendships, ministries and business connections, for I am free from the grips of offense and its stronghold affects. I am delivered in my soul and cover under the blood of the Lamb.

I declare it so! In Jesus name.

Order My Steps

The steps of a good man are order by the Lord: and he delighted in his way.

Psalm 37:23

Lord, your word says that the steps of a good man are order by the Lord; so I declare now, that my steps are being directed in the way that I should go according to your divine will and purpose for my life. Guide me every step of the way so that I will not go a stray. Let your word be a compass in my journey so that, I won't get lost along the way.

Order my steps to go through the right doors, keep my steps on the right path which is according to your divine plan for my life, connecting me to those I'm to be in covenant with. Keep me in your path of righteousness, lead me not into temptation, and deliver me from evil. Guide and direct my steps Lord with the light of your word.

Personal Notes

You prepare a table before me in the presence of my enemies; You anoint my head with oil; my cup runs over.

~The Lords Prayer~

*Our Father Who is in heaven, hallowed be
your name.
Your kingdom come, your will be done on
earth as it is in heaven.
Give us this day our daily bread.*

*And forgive us our debts, as we also have
forgiven left, remitted, and let go of the
debts, and have given up resentment against
our debtors.*

*And lead (bring) us not into temptation, but
deliver us from the evil one. For yours is the
kingdom and the power and the glory
forever. Amen.*

Matthew 6:9-13 (AMP)

*I declare that the will of the Lord, shall be
done in me, on the earth, as it is in heaven. I
shall receive my (provision) bread every
day, and be loaded daily with benefits.*

My debts are forgiven as I forgive my debtors. I am delivered from temptation and evil.

Thank you Lord for perfecting those things which concerns me in my everyday life: spiritually, physically, financially, relationships, ministry and business affairs.

Take a Selah Moment...

Personal Notes

O God, You are my God; early will I seek You; my soul thirsts for You, my flesh longs for You, in a dry place, where no water is...

Personal Notes

Purge me with hyssop, and I shall be clean:
wash me, and I shall be whiter than snow.

Personal Notes

A soft answer turns away wrath: but grievous words stir up anger. Proverbs 15:1

Personal Notes

*"This is the day that the Lord has made, I
will rejoice and be glad in it"*

About the Author

Apostle Vanzant Luster has been chosen for this end time with an apostolic/prophetic mantle, not only has she been called to cities, but nations for this Kingdom age.

She has birthed many spiritual sons and daughters who are now Teachers, Pastors, Evangelists, Prophets, and Apostles.

Apostle Vanzant has attended the School of the Apostles and Prophets. The making of this apostle of God took 46 years and today at the age of 57, He is still making and forming this woman of God for His Glory.

Apostle Vanzant was ordained and licensed into the apostolic office in 2001 by Apostle's Paul and Ida Thornton of Kingdom Dominion International ministry, out of Marietta, Ga.

For more information on Apostolic Flame International Networking Ministries write us at <u>apostolicflameprophetic@gmail.com</u>

Or call...
Ministry Contact number: 404-585-8396

Apostle Vanzant Luster is founder and visionary of Apostle Flame International Networking Ministries. She is also, founder of - Elijah Institute of the Prophets, Women of Wisdom Connections

She is Author, Publisher, Counselor, Mentor, and a Spiritual Mother to many. Radio talk show host and Entrepreneur.

You can listen to Apostle Vanzant's powerful, provoking and sometimes controversial radio broadcast, by simply dialing… 323-843-6067 and you will be connected to a live radio broadcast.

"After Hours Reality Talk"

Every Monday night at… 8:00 P.M. Est.

Apostle Vanzant is the author of the following books...

Man Formed From the Dust of the Ground

21st Century Kingdom Leaders

Disease Issues of the Soul

Kingdom Language

Order in the House

End Time Arsenal

Wrong Decisions

Perils of Wisdom

Caution!

Books can be purchase by going to our website.
www.apostolickingdom.org

Made in the USA
Charleston, SC
20 April 2014